FROM EDGEWOOD TO ETERNITY

Convinced by the Evidence

Ross Thompson

UrbanPress
PUBLISHING YOUR DREAMS

From Edgewood to Eternity
By Ross Thompson
Copyright ©2024 Ross Thompson

ISBN # 978-1-63360-277-9

For Worldwide Distribution
Printed in the U.S.A.

Urban Press
P.O. Box 8881
Pittsburgh, PA 15221-0881
412.646.2780

Table of CONTENTS

Introduction   **vii**

Chapter 1
Where it all began   **1**

Chapter 2
Stones of Remembrance   **5**

Chapter 3
KnotHole Club   **11**

Chapter 4
Shacks Rocks from Easta Pocka   **16**

Chapter 5
Easter Chicks   **20**

Chapter 6
Magic Tricks   **25**

Chapter 7
A Princeton Graduate   **30**

Chapter 8
Unforgettable Claim   **35**

Chapter 9
Shot from a Cannon   **42**

Chapter 10
Gradual Changes   **48**

Chapter 11
Brothers from a Different Father   **53**

Chapter 12
Eventful Road Trip   **58**

Chapter 13
Empty as a Positive   **64**

Chapter 14
Close the Sale   **69**

This book is dedicated to my wife and
best friend – Linda Thompson – and
to our blended families of children,
grandchildren, and great grandchildren.

INTRODUCTION

When I think back to my childhood, I remember one particular incident that was extremely troubling when I was five or six. I can still recall how upset and hurt I was, and the gigantic tears I shed because of the name the boys were calling me. I was playing in Donny Waugaman's backyard, about a block away from our house on East End Avenue in Edgewood. I can't recollect why they began, but in spite of my protests, they just continued calling me that name. I broke out in tears in front of them, walked out of the yard and into the alley. They followed me … taunted me … laughing and saying it all the louder. I couldn't take any more of their name calling, so I ran home through the Saunders' back yard. Imagine how upset I was because they were calling me "a human being." How terrible! I yelled back, "I am *not* a human being."

At home, my mother comforted me, asked what was wrong, and to the best of my recollection, never laughed as she explained what a human being was. My sister Rebecca still laughs at the thought of that traumatic moment in my life. And after all these years, so do I.

Sometimes we react to situations and make decisions without the knowledge of the truth. Had I known what the term "human being" meant, it would not have been troubling. The importance of finding the facts also applies to our faith journey. My purpose for writing this book is in the hope that those who read it will find undeniable evidence to support their faith. Our walk with God is not in a fictional land of make-believe. Instead, our walk is based on facts, with historical evidence to support the life, crucifixion, and resurrection of Jesus Christ.

Each chapter begins with a story from my life experience. These anecdotes are intended to illustrate a point which I will categorize here as either a 'biblical truth' or a 'historical fact.' I define a biblical truth as a statement I **believe** to be true based on my understanding of the Bible. An historical fact is an event that is based on **evidence** from multiple sources and is accepted by scholars.

The first five chapters largely reflect my belief in biblical truths. Beginning in Chapter 6, the content shifts to the historical facts surrounding the Resurrection that are accepted by New Testament scholars and commentators, some of whom are even atheists. Skeptics and those who ridicule Christianity aren't taking into account what history proves to be true. As you read, may your faith be bolstered and your boldness to share the gospel increase. And yes, you are a human being.

CHAPTER 1

Where It All Began

Edgewood is a small community located seven miles east of downtown Pittsburgh. When I grew up in the '50s, it had a population of about 5,000 within the .6 square miles it covered. It's the same town where my parents grew up and graduated from high school. Edgewood Presbyterian is the church where my parents eventually met, were married, and where my two sisters and I were baptized. Our family attended the 11:00 Sunday worship service and sat in the same pew each week—the second pew from the front, on the right side. By sitting so far forward where others could see us, I never gave it a thought to fall asleep.

In the '50s, our church had an award for those who attended Sunday School. If you had perfect attendance, you received a gold lapel pin. And each year thereafter, there were additional awards for perfect attendance that attached to this pin: a wreath around the center pin for year two, and a small gold bar that hung underneath for each successive year. When I graduated from high school, my pin had 12 years of perfect attendance. You might say I'm a Christian because my family went to church and I had 12 years of perfect attendance.

Yes, I grew up in the church, but only a portion of my faith journey had to do with Edgewood Presbyterian. There are three events that come to mind about my journey. The first did involve my church. I remember sitting in the rear of the church basement during the brief assembly before Sunday School when I was seven or eight. As the associate pastor began to pray toward the end of the session, I recall praying his words softly, addressing them to God. Although we said nightly prayers before going to bed, that was the first time I felt I was praying directly to God.

The second influencing factor was my mother. As a child, she grew up in that same church. As an adult, her hunger for spiritual things grew to the point where during the early '60s, she sought God earnestly. She committed her life to the Lord, began to study the Bible, went to a weekly prayer meeting in Mt. Lebanon, and lived an exemplary life for each of her children to see. I remember when she asked me to pray with her at the end of my junior year in high school—to pray for my trip to Argentina that summer of 1966 where I would live with an

Argentine family. I learned to speak and understand Spanish during the three months I was an exchange student in La Rioja, Argentina.

The third event took place in the fall of 1966 when I went to a Young Life weekend retreat at Laurelville Mennonite Campground in Mount Pleasant, PA. That weekend I prayed for Jesus to come into my life and that prayer changed me. For the first time, the Bible made sense. I had a new-found joy, felt more comfortable with myself, and wanted to know more about God and serve him.

POINT
TO
PONDER

When we follow God, we are his children. The faith of our parents doesn't transfer to or cover us. God has no grandchildren. Each of us can have a personal relationship with Him and grow in our own faith.

CHAPTER 2

Stones of Remembrance

I have never questioned God's existence. For as long as I can remember, I had a sense that there is a God. For some, God's existence is a question with which to grapple. *Is there really a God?* There are arguments based on logic that attempt to prove there is a God. And those with opposing viewpoints also argue passionately against it. For me, the single clearest arguments for God's existence are the world and its physical properties. How could such sophisticated building blocks like DNA, or the complexity of the eye that focuses on objects near and far, or the ear that detects noise, or the variety of joints found in the knee, shoulder, and elbow, have just evolved?

The fall weekend retreat with Young Life marked a significant turning point in my life. It was a time when I moved from knowing about God to a place where I believed I had an experience with Him. On Friday night, I prayed with Susie Hill, a Young Life volunteer, and asked Jesus into my life. During the message on Saturday night by the Young Life leader, Reid Carpenter, I wept for 15-20 minutes, not knowing why. Somehow, I received a great emotional release and noticed I was much more comfortable around others. When I came home from that retreat, I felt different. When I read the Bible, things that once had been a mystery made sense. It was as if someone lifted the blinders from my eyes and I was reading with new insight. No one prepped me about what to expect. It just happened. The Holy Spirit opened my eyes.

I've wanted to serve God ever since that weekend. For years, I've journaled about my walk with Him, writing down my struggles, my feelings of discouragement, my questions, and the things I've learned. My desire has been to grow in my faith. Ever since that Young Life weekend, I've never questioned God's presence or existence. In Joshua 4:9, the children of Israel took 12 stones from the Jordan River to be used to make a memorial, so their children and future generations would remember what God had done. These are sometimes referred to as the "stones of remembrance." I look back at that weekend as one of my stones of remembrance. It's important to look back at specific events in our life and remember them as ways God provided for us, met our needs, or performed what seems like a miracle. Four events serve as stones of remembrance for me:

1. **Young Life Weekend**. That weekend retreat in 1966 is when I prayed for God to come into my life. That put me on a new road to follow God.

2. **Prayer with Pastor Russell Bixler**. In the summer after my freshman year of college, Russell Bixler, founder of Cornerstone Television in Pittsburgh, prayed for me on a Sunday night following a prayer and praise meeting in his church. As he prayed, the feeling of an electrical charge went through my arms and hands. It only subsided when I lifted them upward in praise to God. I had a new fervor for God following this prayer.

3. **My job at Lane Furniture.** After selling Keller bedroom and dining room furniture for five years, I nearly quit the furniture industry to sell Shaklee vitamins full time. I'd experienced moderate success in selling Shaklee products in my free time, and was discouraged

by the way the salesmen were treated at Keller. I prayed long and hard for direction and guidance. In the midst of searching, I called my friend John Hart, a fellow Keller representative, for advice. While talking with him, he urged me to attend the upcoming October furniture show (furniture market) in High Point, North Carolina, where I could look for another opportunity. I took his advice and attended.

During the show, someone I knew mentioned he had applied for a job opening at Action Industries (Lane Furniture). I wasn't even aware of what Action Industries sold. I did a little research, discovered they were growing rapidly, interviewed for the job, and started with them on December 1, 1984. To my surprise, many of those with whom I worked were Christians. It was at Lane where I developed life-long relationships with other Christian men.

4. **"I will see you through."** Shortly after my marital separation in 2012, I went to one of the chapels in Allegheny Center Alliance

Church, which was my home church. I spent more than an hour praying, weeping, and lying prostrate on the floor. I then sat at the rear of the chapel and continued praying. While there, I had a strong sense that God was saying, "I will see you through." There wasn't an audible voice, but I felt God was speaking to me—encouraging me—and reassuring me that he would walk with me through difficulties.

POINT
TO
PONDER

As you reflect on your own life, what are your
stones of remembrance? What experiences can
you look back and hold on to so you can be
confident in God and your relationship with
Him? These stones may be important turning
points. Remembering those stones will give
you assurance and peace of mind.

CHAPTER 3

Knothole Club

Growing up in Western Pennsylvania, I've always been a fan of the Pittsburgh Pirates. I have fond memories of taking my three boys to see the Pirates battle the Mets in the late '80s, taunting the Mets' outfielder Daryl Strawberry by chanting "Daryl" along with thousands of other, standing and cheering in front of our right field seats during a playoff game, sitting in seats overlooking left field on Sunday after church, working our way down from the cheap seats in the outfield until we reached the third row near the dugout, the thrill of Andy Van Slyke tossing a ball to Ben as he left the field after catching the final out of an inning, and Jon yelling out to Johnny Ray, "I have your baseball card." We loved the Pirates and were happy to sit anywhere in the stadium as long as we could watch. Anywhere was fine—left field, right field, third base box seats. We just wanted to be there.

My earliest recollection of being at a

Pirates baseball game was when I was eight or nine. Edgewood Borough had a recreation department and one of their summer activities was to take a bus load of kids to Forbes Field to cheer on the Pirates on a Saturday afternoon. For a few dollars, 40 or 50 of us packed into a school bus with our needed supplies in hand: a baseball glove and an Isaly's chipped/chopped ham sandwich in a brown paper bag. Once we arrived at Forbes Field, we were told to remember our bus number and return to the same spot after the game. We needed to remember that number because there were 20 or more identical school buses unloading kids in the parking area outside the center field wall.

I don't recall being supervised by any adult. It's a miracle we never lost anyone. We just got off the bus as we were instructed to do, walked to the outfield entrance, showed them our "Knothole Club" card at the gate, entered for free, and scrambled to the right field seats so we could watch number 21. In the late '50s, we had no idea we were just a few feet away from one of baseball's greatest players, namely Roberto Clemente. We would shout and cheer for Roberto as he warmed up before the game. He smiled and made gestures back to us. We loved watching him and dreamed of one day becoming a Pirate. All we knew is that we wanted to be there in Forbes Field—anywhere in Forbes Field—just to see our Pirates.

Thinking about the Pirates makes me recall how much we wanted to be there, how we sat in various sections in the stadium, and used a number of entrances to get in. That's similar to our spiritual journey. When this life is over, we want to be there with God, to have our name listed in the Book of Life, and to hear, "Well done, good and faithful servant." How we entered into God's kingdom will be different for each of us. We just want to be there.

In my case, I had an experience to which I can look back and determine when I began to follow the Lord. Others may have had a dramatic story like the conversion of Paul, where his life was turned completely upside down. Many of those I know have grown up in the church and can never remember a time when they didn't believe in God, or exactly when they started to believe. No matter how we get there, what indicates that we are a Christian is that we can confess what we find in Romans 10:9, "If you declare with your mouth that Jesus is Lord, and believe in your heart that God raised him from the dead, you will be saved."

This verse is believed to be an early creed of the church. It is thought to have been a confession of faith and repeated by those who were being baptized. There are three parts to that verse: 1) declaring with your mouth that Jesus is Lord of your life; 2) believing that He died; and 3) believing He was resurrected to life. Belief in the resurrection of Jesus is one of the earliest confessions about Jesus. It is also one of the cornerstones of the faith. Without the Resurrection, Christianity leaves us hopeless.

POINT
TO
PONDER

Each of us has our own, unique story as to how we became a Christian. For some it could be a dramatic story. For others, an uneventful one. Your story isn't what determines whether you are a Christian. It's your confession that Jesus is Lord and your belief in His resurrection that seals your inheritance in the Kingdom.

CHAPTER 4

Shacks Rocks from Easta Pocka

A Figment of My Imagination

As a six or seven-year-old, I loved to play "cowboys and Indians" with Donny and Bobby Waugaman, Billy Swift, Dennis Wahl, and others in my Regent Square neighborhood. Some of us would act as the bad guys and steal an imaginary treasure of gold. The rest would shoot them with our guns in an effort to retrieve the gold. But our pretend bullets never hit the bad guys. They always got away with the stolen gold. By the time I was six, I had already been playing 'cowboys' at home for a year or two. Watching the Lone Ranger and his Indian side-kick Tonto on Saturday mornings on our black and white TV had already influenced me. When I played as a cowboy at home, I called myself "Shacks Rocks from Easta Pocka." I have no idea where I came upon that name, but the name made me feel strong and powerful, even though the cowboy I portrayed was imaginary.

There are some who think the same way about Jesus … that he is some imaginary and powerless figure who never lived. A survey by the Barna Group for the Church of England in 2015 found that 22% of adults living in the UK did not believe that Jesus was a real historical figure.[1] It's a surprising percentage for 2 in 9 adults to question his existence, and stands in contrast to the credentialed scholars who unanimously believe he lived. Fortunately, today we stand at a point in time where so much data supports our belief that Jesus walked among us.

For those who question the historicity of Jesus—as to whether he is a genuine historical figure—there are multiple non-biblical sources. Below is a partial list of Greek and Roman writers and historians who mentioned Jesus and his followers in their writings. They may not give us a lot of detail about him, but their reference gives great credibility that he lived and walked among us.

- Tacitus – Roman historian who authored "*Annals of Imperial Rome*" around AD 116, a work which records the burning of Rome, that Emperor Nero blamed Christians for it, and that Jesus was put to death by Pontius Pilate.

- Pliny the Younger – Roman governor who wrote to Emperor Trajan around AD 112, seeking advice about Christians who would "sing hymns to Christ as a god."

- Flavius Josephus – Jewish historian who wrote *Antiquities of the Jews* around AD 93. In the 20-volume work, he twice mentions Jesus.

- Suetonius (AD 69 to AD 122) – Roman historian and court official who wrote the biographies of 12 Roman rulers and references Jesus twice in his writings.

- Lucian of Samosata (AD 115 to AD 180) – A second-century Greek satirist who mocked Jesus' followers in his writings.

- Babylonian Talmud – most likely compiled between AD 70 and AD 300, an important Jewish work that confirms Jesus' crucifixion.

POINT
TO
PONDER

Without a doubt, Jesus lived. There are so many independent attestations of Jesus' existence that it is actually "astounding for an ancient figure of any kind."[2]

[1] *Talking Jesus*, a 2015 study by the Barna Group on behalf of the Church of England, Evangelical Alliance, and HOPE.

[2] *"Did Jesus Exist?"* by Bart D. Ehrman article in *Huffington Post,* April 8, 2014.

CHAPTER 5

Easter Chicks

The One That Didn't Die a Second Time

I have two distinct memories that mark my first exposure to the fleeting nature of life. In the '50s, it was commonplace for families to get a baby chicken called a chick for Easter. These chicks had their feathers dyed blue, green, orange, or some other color, and were intended to be a short-term pet for curious children. Often their lives were brief due to lack of food, improper care, or unintended abuse. My first encounter with death was at the expense of an Easter chick. I don't remember the cause of its demise, but I do remember giving it a proper burial in our backyard next to our garage. I also made sure it had a headstone, a small wood board with the name this chick carried for a few weeks.

Just a few years later, a second death

impacted my life in a far more significant way: the death of my grandmother, Louise Creelman. When she died, I was at Camp Twin Echo, a Boy Scout summer camp. Thinking they were doing the right thing, my parents allowed me to stay for the entire week and work on my advancements. Only when I returned home did I discover my Nana was gone. I was upset, disappointed, and didn't know how to handle the sadness within me. I was angry because I never got a chance to give her a proper good-bye. Even to this day, when I think of my Nana, I have a sense of loss.

There's one death that had a far greater impact than either of these first two. The death of a chick fades within a few days. The loss of a grandmother can last a lifetime. But the death of Jesus affects all eternity for each and every one of us. Jesus suffered a horrendous death, marked by agonizing torture, whipping by a stone-studded rope, flesh being torn from his body with wounds revealing internal organs, terrible abuse to his body, and a death that ended with suffocation. Yet, in spite of all his suffering, we look beyond his death and focus on his resurrection. It is the resurrection that separates his death from all others and gives us hope.

The Bible has nine accounts of people who died and were brought back to life.[3] Of those nine, eight came back to life and then died a second time. In all of history, only Jesus was resurrected from the dead—permanently, never again to die. Paul writes a letter to the Corinthian church in which he addresses the resurrection. In the 1 Corinthians 15, he says the following,

- Christ died for our sins, just as the Scriptures said. He was buried and he was raised from the dead on the third day, just as the Scriptures said. (1 Corinthians 15:3-4)

- And if Christ has not been raised, then all our preaching is useless, and your faith is useless. And we apostles would all be lying about God—for we have said that God raised Christ from the grave. (1 Corinthians 15:14-15)

- But in fact, Christ has been raised from the dead. He is the first of a great harvest of all who have died. (1 Corinthians 15:20)

Paul writes with great conviction that Jesus was resurrected. There are more than 300 verses in the New Testament on the Resurrection. The Christian faith depends on this event. If the resurrection never happened, then our belief is in a lie and pointless. In the New Testament, everything comes back to the Resurrection as the center of doctrine and practice.

Recently I found the journal entry I made on January 13, 2014, after reading Romans 6. I was overwhelmed by the importance of the res-urrection in a way it hadn't struck me before. My entry reads, "This is no game … no philo-sophical argument. Christ was raised from the dead … shocking … unbelievable … powerful. How can his deity be denied if He is raised from the dead? And how can those who know that truth deny he is Lord." I often look back to that January day and clearly remember the chair and the room in which I was sitting. I wondered, *Why doesn't this truth cause huge excitement among believers? Why don't we shout it from the roof tops?* That day sparked the beginning of my quest to learn more about the Resurrection, which has recently been fueled by the work of Dr. Gary Habermas.

POINT
TO
PONDER

Jesus' Resurrection is at the core of the Gospel, with over 300 New Testament verses in reference to it.

[3]Bible accounts of those who died and brought back to life include:

1. The son of the Zarephath widow (1 Kings 17:17-22)
2. The son of a Shunammite woman (2 Kings 4:32-35)
3. A dead man thrown into Elisha's tomb (2 Kings 13:20-21)
4. Jesus (Matthew 28:5-8)
5. The son of the widow in Nain (Luke 7:11-15)
6. The daughter of Jairus (Luke 8:41-42, 49-55)
7. Lazarus (John 11:1-44)
8. Dorcas (Acts 9:36-41)
9. Eutychus (Acts 20:9-10)

CHAPTER 6

Magic Tricks

Introduction to the Six Facts

As a ten-year-old, I loved performing magic tricks. *Where did the little black ball go? It was in the small plastic vase before your eyes a moment ago.* When I covered it, said the magic word "abracadabra," and waved my magic wand, the ball disappeared. I also had the special ability to change a dime into a nickel, and then back again. If you'd like a card trick, just pull one from the deck, look at it, and put it back. Even after shuffling the deck, I could pick out your chosen card.

When I grew older, I still enjoyed the appearance of a magic trick in my sales meetings. Part of my job as a sales representative for Lane was to train store salespeople in selling our product. One of my favorite attention getters was to use a book titled *A Fun Magic Coloring Book* at the beginning of the presentation. It used the same principle as the magic deck of cards. Both sides of the card are shaved slightly at one end, while the other end is not. By doing so, it gives the card a slight "v" shape so it is wider at one end than the other. When a card is chosen, the deck is turned before putting it back in. When the card is placed with the others, it's wider than the rest and can easily be slid out of the deck, with the appearance of being magically found.

The *Fun Magic Coloring Book* uses a similar method and is cut so there are three ways to flip the pages. Flipping the pages from the bottom reveals only blank, white pages. Flipping it from the middle reveals pages with images that are only outlined in black and white. Flipping pages from the top reveals fully colored pictures within the black and white outlines. It's a great attention getter and generates questions like, "How did you do that?" The illusion accomplishes its purpose.

Some skeptics speculate the resurrection of Jesus is a similar illusion and never happened. Maybe the disciples stole the body to make it appear he rose, and disposed of it elsewhere. Or possibly, he didn't actually die, but escaped, and lived his life elsewhere. Could it be that all this talk of the resurrection is just a legend that grew over time? Can anyone prove the resurrection?

One man has dedicated his professional career toward those ends. Dr. Gary Habermas is a distinguished research professor of apologetics and philosophy at Liberty University in Lynchburg, Virginia. He has written numerous books, lectures throughout the U.S., and produced scores of videos which are available on YouTube.[4] His life's work has been to examine the relevant historical, philosophical, and theological issues surrounding the death and resurrection of Jesus. In 1976, he began the development of his Minimal Facts Argument. He writes,

> This approach has two major steps, and it has been pointed out at length that the initial stage is easily the most crucial. 1) No historical or other fact will be employed unless it can be established by multiple lines of evidence, each being derived by critical means. Because of this initial underpinning, 2) virtually all recent critical scholars, including atheists, agnostics, and other skeptical specialists in relevant fields, accept these facts.[5]

With this basis for establishing his six facts, it is understandable why even atheist and agnostics agree the statements are true. Below are the six facts: [6]

> Fact #1: Jesus died by Roman crucifixion
>
> Fact #2: The disciples saw something they believed to be the risen Jesus

Fact #3: They immediately began preaching

Fact #4: The disciples were overjoyed and their lives totally transformed

Fact #5: James, Jesus' brother, is one of two skeptics whose life was transformed when he claimed he saw the risen Christ

Fact #6: Paul, a Jewish zealot, is the other skeptic whose life was transformed when he claimed he met the risen Christ on the road to Damascus.[6]

Dr. Gary Habermas states,

The Minimal Facts Argument reduces the boulders behind which skeptics hide with their critiques of the resurrection. One by one the boulders are removed, leaving them with few come-backs against the resurrection.[7]

POINT
TO
PONDER

Biblical scholars who have studied the historical facts about Jesus agree that the six minimal facts are true. Surprisingly, these scholars include agnostics and even atheists. Each one of these facts is a clue that, when considered together, lead one to conclude the Resurrection actually occurred.

[4] Gary Habermas has written more than 20 books, including *The Case for the Resurrection of Jesus (2004); Did the Resurrection Happen? A Conversation with Gary Habermas and Anthony Flew (2009); Evidence for the Historical Jesus (2020); Risen Indeed: A Historical Investigation into the Resurrection of Jesus (2021)*

[5] Gary Habermas, *Risen Indeed: A Historical Investigation into the Resurrection of Jesus* (Lexham Academic, 2021), pages 21-22.

[6] Gary Habermas, *Do We Have Actual Evidence for the Resurrection of Jesus?*, Alicia Childers interview on YouTube, August 12, 2022.

[7] Gary Habermas, *What's Happening in Resurrection Trends,* 10/1/22 YouTube video.

CHAPTER 7

A Princeton Graduate

Fact #1: Jesus died by Roman crucifixion.

My father, Ross W. Thompson, graduated from Princeton University in 1932. My father and Jimmy Stewart, the actor best known for his character George Bailey in the 1946 film *It's a Wonderful Life*, were in the same graduating class. If a person was to challenge that my father graduated from Princeton, I could use several methods to prove it is a historical fact. I could produce his diploma from Princeton as one source. A second source would be his 1932 yearbook that contains his picture and name. A third item would be a picture of his class on the steps of one of the campus buildings. Sworn testimony from those who knew him, and his three children in particular, would be a fourth source.

Biblical scholars use similar methods to verify a historical fact. They use 1) the best kind, which was eyewitness testimony, recorded close to the event and is referred to as "early"; 2) multiple attestation, which is data from more than one source to support the fact; 3) written documents like letters and recorded history; 4) archeological evidence; 5) information that might be embarrassing or unlikely to be recorded giving credence to a fact; and 6) and enemy attestation that might view the event in a negative way. Historical reliability is supported when there are at least two sources. Four or more sources indicates the fact is highly reliable.

The next few chapters expand on the six facts that Gary Habermas presents as the best evidence for the resurrection of Jesus. Credentialed biblical scholars who have studied the New Testament and earned a master's or doctoral degree or completed additional studies agree that these six historical facts are true. In a lecture series given at the Billy Graham Training Center at the Cove, Gary Habermas states that there are 17 ancient sources that fit this criterion to show that Jesus was a historical figure.[8] According to Habermas, one of the main facts we know about Jesus is his crucifixion. Bart Ehrman, an atheist biblical scholar, sites 15 independent sources from within 100 years of Jesus' death on the cross, including (all emphasis added is mine),

- All four gospels: Matthew, Mark, Luke, and John

- Josephus (AD 90) writes, "When Pilate, upon hearing him accused by men of the highest standing amongst us, had **condemned him to be crucified**"

- Tacitus (AD 120) reports, "Nero fastened the guilt [of the burning of Rome] and inflicted the **most exquisite torture** on a class hated for their abominations, called Christians by the populace. Christus, from whom the name had its origins, suffered the extreme penalty during the reign of Tiberius at the hands of one of our procurators, Pontius Pilate."

- Lucian of Samosata (AD 170), the Greek satirist wrote, "The Christians, you know, worship a man to this day—the distinguished personage who introduced their novel rites, and was **crucified** on that account."

- Mara Bar-Serapion, (AD 73) writing to his son from prison comments, "Or [what advantage came to] the Jews by **the murder** of their Wise King, seeing that from that very time their kingdom was driven away from them?" Although Mara Bar-Serapion does not mention crucifixion as the mode of Jesus' execution, he does say that he was killed.

- The Talmud (AD 70 to AD 200) is a good example of "enemy attestation." The following statement serves as support of his crucifixion when it says "on the eve of the Passover *Yeshu was hanged*." Yeshu is the name Joshua in Hebrew and the equivalent in Greek to Jesus as he was "hung" on the cross.[9]

POINT
TO
PONDER

Clearly, Jesus' death by crucifixion is a
historical fact and supported by a considerable
number of biblical and non-biblical sources.
Even atheist New Testament scholars accept
his crucifixion as a historical fact. This is Gary
Habermas' Fact #1, the first clue.

[8] Gary Habermas, *Facts for the Resurrection of Jesus* – Lecture
series by Gary Habermas given at the Billy Graham Training
Center – YouTube.

[9] Gary Habermas, *The Case for the Resurrection of Jesus* (Kregel
Publications, 2004), all five quotes, page 49.

CHAPTER 8

Unforgettable Claim

Fact #2: The disciples saw something they believed to be the risen Jesus.

When I was a seventh grader, I was accused of vandalizing school property after dismissal at 3:45 and that the damage was worthy of punishment. Hearing the claim that someone saw me do it shocked me. I couldn't figure out what I might have done and what they saw that would warrant my facing the school principal. I rarely got into trouble. I was a Boy Scout and the twelve points of the Scout Law were indelibly written on my mind, so much so that I can still recite it today from memory. "A Scout is trustworthy, loyal, helpful, friendly, courteous, kind, obedient, cheerful, thrifty, brave, clean, and reverent." Nowhere in that law is permission given to vandalize school property.

Later I was told someone had confused me with another boy. We had a similar build and short, reddish hair styled in a crew cut. He was the one who misbehaved and received the appropriate reprimand. Apparently, he didn't take the Scout Law as seriously because we were both in Troop 23. I do not remember what he did, but I'll never forget being identified as the culprit and the relief I felt when the error was acknowledged.

As in my situation, sometimes witnesses see things and are incorrect in processing what they saw. The disciples saw **something** after Jesus' death. They claimed they saw the risen Jesus, but were they correct? Or were they mistaken? The claim in itself does not prove he was raised from the dead, but their unanimous agreement indicates there's reasonable certainty they saw something. The disciples used the language of sight—*they saw something*. Some doubt the claim, suggesting instead they must have been hallucinating. That argument doesn't explain away their claim because it's not possible that two or three people have the identical hallucination, let alone the 500 mentioned in 1 Corinthians 15. Is it possible the disciples saw nothing, but agreed to make this claim? If so, for what purpose? None of the disciples recanted, even though they suffered persecution and even death. It's fair to conclude they did see something.

The four gospels, the book of Acts, and Paul's first letter to the Corinthians each give accounts of people seeing the risen Jesus. In total, eleven separate events are reported. The gospels and Acts contain nine of the events.[10] Of the nine, seven events are mentioned in more than one source. The Easter account is found in all four gospels. Below is a small sampling:

- Matthew writes, "Then the eleven disciples went to Galilee, to the mountain where Jesus had told them to go. When they saw him, they worshiped him" (Matthew 28:16-17).

- The last chapter of Mark describes the story of Mary Magdalene and the two women who go to Jesus' tomb. They are met there by an angel who tells them Jesus is risen from the dead. They are to tell the disciples that Jesus "is going ahead of you into Galilee. There you will see him" (Mark 16:1-7).

- Luke records the story of two of Jesus' followers who met Jesus following his crucifixion, while they walked to Emmaus (see Luke 24:13-34). A few verses later, Jesus appears to his disciples and says, "Why are you frightened?" he asked. "Why are your hearts filled with doubt? Look at my hands. Look at my feet. You can see that it's really me" (Luke 24:38).

- In John, Mary Magdalene found the disciples and told them, "I have seen the Lord." (John 20:18) The disciples told Thomas, "We have seen the Lord" (20:25). And later in John, Jesus himself says, "You believe because you have seen me. Blessed are those who believe without seeing me" (John 20:29).

- The first among many sermons recorded in Acts is given by Peter in which he stated, "You killed the author of life, but God raised him from the dead. We are witnesses of this" (Acts 3:15).

In addition to the gospels, the writings of Paul support the claim that the disciples saw the risen Christ. Biblical scholars accept several books as authentically written by Paul because he was a scholar, a Jewish Pharisee, and a zealot intent on doing his part to eradicate Christianity. These seven include Romans, 1 Corinthians, 2 Corinthians, Galatians, Philippians, 1 Thessalonians, and Philemon.

Immediately after Paul's conversion in

AD 32 or AD 33, he went into Arabia. Three years later, he went to Jerusalem in order to get to know Peter and James, Jesus' brother. Paul spent 15 days there, making sure he was preaching the same good news as the others were. It is believed that during this time Paul received the early creed found in 1 Corinthians 15:3-8. This indicates the creed was in circulation before his conversion, and most scholars believe within two years of the crucifixion. As cited in Chapter 5, James D. G. Dunn, a prominent New Testament scholar, believes this creed could go back even further—to within two months of Jesus' death. This early Corinthian creed records five distinct sightings of the risen Lord:

- "He appeared to Cephas (Peter), and then to the Twelve" (verse 5)
- "After that, he appeared to more than five hundred of the brothers and sisters at the same time, most of whom are still living" (verse 6)
- "Then he appeared to James" (verse 7)
- "Then to all the apostles" (verse 7)
- "Last of all, he appeared to me also" (verse 8).

After 14 more years (about AD 50), Paul, along with Barnabas and Titus, returned to Jerusalem to confirm for a second time the gospel he preached was in agreement with that of the other apostles. While there, he conferred with the leaders of the church, including Peter, James, and this time John. An important component of the gospel is that the resurrected Jesus was seen following his crucifixion. Paul writes, "The leaders of the church had nothing to add to what I was preaching" (see Galatians 2:1-6).

Lastly, a third source supporting the claim that the risen Jesus was seen is the apostolic fathers who succeeded the apostles and may have fellowshiped with them. The apostolic fathers taught that the apostles were dramatically impacted by Jesus' resurrection.[11] These included Clement (AD 35-AD 110) and Polycarp (AD 69-AD 155). They had conversations with and wrote about the apostles who had witnessed Jesus' death and resurrection.

[10]The eleven events where Jesus was seen:
1. At the empty tomb (Matthew 28:1-10; Mark 16:1-8; Luke 24:1-12; John 20:1-9)
2. Mary Magdalene at the tomb (Mark 16:9-11; John 20:11-18)
3. Two travelers to Emmaus (John 24:13-32)
4. Peter in Jerusalem (Luke 24:13-32; 1 Corinthians 15:5)
5. Ten disciples in the upper room (Mark 16:14; Luke 24:36-43; John 20:19-25)
6. Eleven disciples in the upper room (John 20:26-31; 1 Corinthians 15:5)

POINT
TO
PONDER

The gospels and the book of Acts report multiple accounts of interactions with the resurrected Jesus. They touched him, ate with him, and conversed with him. Paul's letters, the creeds, and the writings of the early church fathers also support the claim that the resurrected Jesus was seen by the disciples. This is Fact #2, the second clue in support of Jesus' resurrection.

7. Seven disciples fishing on the Sea of Galilee (John 21:1-23)
8. Eleven disciples on the mountain in Galilee (Matthew 28:16-20; Mark 16:15-16)
9. More than 500 (1 Corinthians 15:6)
10. James (1 Corinthians 15:7)
11. The Ascension at the Mount of Olives (Luke 24:44-49; Acts 1:3-8)

[11] Gary Habermas, *The Case for the Resurrection of Jesus* (Kregel Publications, 2004), page 53.

CHAPTER 9

Shot from a Cannon

Fact #3: They began preaching immediately.

I was born in 1949, four years after the end of World War II. For much of the previous decade, the war abroad and our military influenced everyday life. Dad sometimes spoke of gas rationing and how rubber tires were scarce during the war. He and Mom were able to save and acquire enough gas coupons to travel to Berea, Kentucky for their honeymoon in 1942. My mom remembered her meal planning, keeping the rationing of sugar, meat, and even butter in mind. Sales of commodities like shoes, soap, and coffee were also regulated. Women became heroes by working as welders, machine operators, and factory workers in jobs previously held by the boys who were serving abroad.

When the war was over, its influence could still be felt. Returning soldiers got involved in Boy Scouts and created a disciplined atmosphere for boys that felt somewhat like the army. TV shows like *McHale's Navy*, and Hollywood movies like the submarine thriller *Run Silent, Run Deep*, brought the drama of war before our eyes. Toy stores were filled with a wide variety of miniature tanks, airplanes, missiles, Jeeps, battleships, helicopters, rifles, grenades, army helmets, and even German lugers. I spent hours playing with miniature rubber toy soldiers, complete with rifles, bazookas, and tanks.

One additional toy I had, which had modest popularity in the 1950s, was a cast iron *Big Bang Cannon*. Mine was ten inches long, and bronze colored with red wheels. These cannons operated by introducing a little carbide into a chamber containing some water, where it reacted immediately to release acetylene gas. In a few seconds, gas filled the chamber. I liked hitting the igniter. It created a spark that caused the acetylene gas to explode. The explosion created a deafening bang and a flash of light that came out of the barrel.

Although there wasn't a loud bang, the message of Jesus' resurrection shot out of Jerusalem as if it was from a cannon. The

"explosion" took place a few days after his crucifixion, ignited by a slow burning fuse. On
Friday, Jesus died. Saturday was Black Saturday.
The disciples were depressed and felt a sense
of failure. On Sunday, came the explosion. The
powder that caused the explosion was the resurrection of Jesus. He appeared multiple times
to the disciples during the 40 days following His
crucifixion (see Acts 1:3).

His disciples began preaching very soon
afterward, with the first powerful sermon delivered by Peter about 50 days later at Pentecost.
Acts records some 3,000 became believers following this address, and the explosion had be-
gun to affect many lives. Peter's sermons can
be found in Acts 1-5, 10, and 11. One of Paul's
sermons is in Acts chapter 13. These sermons
define the central beliefs of the gospel.

According to Dr. Gary Habermas, "Few
people knew how to read . . . so they relied on
oral tradition to teach others."[12] Jesus taught
with the use of parables and stories so his message could be remembered. Similarly, the early
Church taught core beliefs to illiterate followers
with the use of creeds that were spoken orally.
Creeds are short, pithy statements that are spoken with a rhythm or cadence and are easy to
memorize. They were repeated frequently so the
gospel could be committed to memory. There are
many creeds found in the New Testament letters
and pre-date the letters in which they are found.

One of the most notable creeds is found in chapter 15 of Paul's first letter to the Corinthians, which was referred to earlier in Chapter 5:

> For what I received I passed on to you as of first importance: that Christ died for our sins according to the Scriptures, that he was buried, that he was raised on the third day according to the Scriptures, and that he appeared to Cephas, and then to the Twelve. After that, he appeared to more than five hundred of the brothers and sisters at the same time, most of whom are still living, though some have fallen asleep. Then he appeared to James, then to all the apostles, and last of all he appeared to me also (1 Corinthians 15:3-7).

The time line of the Creeds is very close to the crucifixion, and the messages are consistent. The early Church creeds almost always include deity, death, and resurrection. With their being formulated so soon after the resurrection, they provide some of the strongest data in support of it. The passage above, "that Christ died for our sins" (verse 3), is a strong indication of Jesus' deity. Who can forgive sins but God? Verse four implies his death by stating, "that he was buried." And being "raised from the dead" describes his resurrection.

There is a new trend in New Testament

scholarship. Within the past few years, scholars realized the disciples believed in Jesus' divinity from the start. Previously, scholars looked at John chapter 1 as the final culmination about Jesus' divinity and that belief in his divinity grew and evolved over time, until AD 95, when the gospel of John was written. However, recent studies of the creeds conclude that the early Church believed in Jesus' deity at the outset. Often creeds refer to Jesus as "Lord." The word *Lord* in Greek is *kurios*, the same word used for God and Christ. The phrase "the earliest Christology was already the highest Christology" is used to describe this new conclusion.[13]

Scholars agree the preaching of the gospel of Jesus Christ began within weeks of his death. The message preached included his deity, death and Resurrection. The core beliefs which were preached are found in the early creeds. The early creeds contained an easily memorized message and originated within a couple years of his death—and possibly even within a few months. There is great consistency in the creeds. No wonder Christianity spread so widely and so quickly.

POINT
TO
PONDER

The early Creeds contain the core message about Jesus' deity, death, and resurrection. Not one of his followers disputed any aspect of the Creeds. Immediately following Jesus' death, the message shot out from Jerusalem as if from a cannon. This is Fact #3 and the third clue pointing to the truth of Jesus' resurrection.

[12] Gary Habermas, *The Case for the Resurrection of Jesus.* Kregel Publications 2004, page 52.

[13] Richard Bauckham, *Jesus and the God of Israel: God Crucified and Other Studies on the New Testament's Christology of Divine Healing (Eerdman's, 2008),* pages 128-130.

CHAPTER 10

Gradual Changes

Fact #4: The disciples were overjoyed and their lives were totally transformed.

When I reflect on who I was in high school, I'm now not the same person I was then. Some say people don't change. I believe changes occurred gradually over time, and I did change. Changes happen for a number of different reasons. Some changes happen as we grow physically and mature. Others happen as we have new life experiences and take on responsibilities, like a job, marriage, or a growing family. Changes often occur when we are no longer willing to put up with something that is painful. Life's difficulties have the unique ability to strengthen, refine, and give us reason to change. As we develop our talents, proficiency increases and we feel differently about ourselves.

As I think about some of the ways I have changed over the years, there are several that comes to mind. I'm not talking about physical changes, like when my sisters laughed hearing my voice crack in junior high. I'm talking about changes in my attitudes, beliefs, actions, and personality. When I was in eighth grade, someone asked if I didn't like people because I hadn't attended a school dance. That question baffled me. I was timid and lacked confidence, but never equated being timid with not liking people.

Although at times I still feel shy in a crowd, my work with Young Life in seminary and a 39-year furniture sales career with Keller and Lane forced me to interact with people and overcome that tendency. I find it interesting that my entire working career in furniture revolved around working with people, thus forcing me to change if I wanted to be effective. I conducted hundreds of sales meetings, educated store employees with information on my product, gave them pointers on how to sell more effectively, and built personal relationships with factory personnel at Keller and Lane, as well as store employees with whom I came in contact. After years of doing my job, no one would accuse me of being timid and afraid of people. In fact, I communicate extremely well, with a group or an individual. It was a gradual process, but change occurred nonetheless.

In the New Testament account, the lives of the disciples were dramatically changed after the crucifixion. Their change wasn't gradual. Their transformation occurred within days of the crucifixion, and gives evidence to support the claim of Jesus' resurrection. When Jesus was arrested, his disciples were afraid and lost hope. Their dream that he was the Messiah was dashed. There's no mention of any disciples watching Jesus' torture or being present while he was on the cross—an indication of their desire to distance themselves from him. On Friday, they all abandoned him. Peter shrunk in fear and denied even knowing Jesus. On Saturday, the confused disciples hid behind locked doors. On Sunday morning, women, rather than disciples, went to his tomb to anoint Jesus' body with burial spices (see Mark 16:1).

Habermas writes, "After Jesus' death, the lives of the disciples were transformed to the point that they endured persecution and even martyrdom."[14] In his letter to the church in Philippi, Polycarp gives an account of the suffering that Peter, Paul and other followers of Jesus endured.[15] What took place for the disciples to be transformed from a fearful band into fearless followers? What gave them the boldness to risk their lives, even to the point of death? It's one thing to claim something happened; it's another to put one's life on the line for that belief. What took place in Peter in a 50-day period? He went from a man who denied knowing Jesus, to one who delivered a compelling sermon after which 3,000 people believed. Aside from Judas who took his own life before the resurrection, historical records and church tradition indicate all of the disciples shared that belief.

Ten of the disciples died as martyrs because of their belief. Only John was not put to death, but suffered greatly for it. Tradition says he ministered in the region around Ephesus in modern day Turkey, and is buried there. Jesus' inner circle of followers were stabbed, beheaded, crucified, sawn in half, struck with a sword, or shot with arrows. Peter and Paul were killed in Rome in AD 66. Although Thomas initially doubted the resurrection, he demonstrated his faith in the risen Jesus by traveling east to Syria, Iraq, and finally to India to spread the gospel. The Marthoma Christians in India consider Thomas to be their founder and their tradition says he died by stabbing at the hands of four soldiers. All of the disciples suffered because of their proclamation of Jesus as Lord.

POINT
TO
PONDER

It's not reasonable to believe that Jesus'
followers risked and gave their lives for
anything other than what they claimed and
believed to be true. The sudden transformation
of the disciples following Jesus' death is Fact
#4. Other than the Resurrection, what other
event could have caused such a radical change?
Their transformation is the 4th clue.

[14]Gary Habermas, *The Case for the Resurrection of Jesus* (Kregel
Publications, 2004), page 53.

[15]Gary Habermas, *The Case for the Resurrection of Jesus* (regel
Publications, 2004), page 57.

CHAPTER 11

Brothers From A Different Father

Fact #5: James, Jesus' brother, was a skeptic whose life was transformed when he saw the risen Christ.

When I worked for Lane Furniture, I developed four lifelong relationships. Larry Sheets, Bobby Spain, Butch Dumbleton, and Jim Blonkowski were my Lane 'brothers.' We lived miles apart in five different states: Ohio, Kentucky, Georgia, Maryland, and Pennsylvania. Yet we had regular contact with each other as we talked by phone on our afternoon drive home from working with our accounts. We called this our "windshield time." Four of us shared a house at the furniture markets in High Point,

NC. When calculated, our foursome spent more than a year of our lives under the same roof.

I shared a special bond with Bobby and Larry. Bobby was an important support for me when I went through some personal difficulties. His listening ear, understanding of similar situations, and wise counsel comforted me. Larry and I connected in a different way. We organized the worship services we conducted at our High Point and Las Vegas showrooms during markets. He was the lead planner. I often led the singing. Larry and I gave our share of messages at the 7:00 a.m. service for our fellow Lane salespeople and marketing staff. I remember one Sunday when I spoke before 70-80 attendees. These were positive gatherings which facilitated in our becoming more transparent and honest with one another. Bobby and Larry were my closest friends and I occasionally called them my brothers from a different mother.

James, a leader in the early church in Jerusalem, was Jesus' brother—but not from another mother. In his case, he was from another father. I imagine it must have been hard growing up with Jesus as an older brother, a brother who was obedient to his parents and did no wrong. How could James live up to the standards set by his brother? And the stories James heard of his brother must have made his head spin.

Among the strange stories James would have heard was the incident when Jesus was 12.

That year, like every other, his parents went to Jerusalem for the Passover festival. As they returned home, they thought Jesus was among the other travelers accompanying them. At nightfall, they looked for but could not find him, so they hastily returned to Jerusalem. After looking for him three days, his parents found Jesus in the Temple, sitting among the religious leaders where he was listening and asking them questions. "His parents didn't know what to think. 'Son' his mother said to him. Why have you done this to us? Your father and I have been frantic, searching for you everywhere. But why did you need to search? he asked. Didn't you know I must be in my Father's house?" (Luke 2:49). Nobody understood what Jesus meant.

As his older brother was in his early 30s, James continued to hear unusual stories, like how Jesus had a band of men following him, how he spun stories to crowds on the hilltop, and even how he disrespected the religious leaders by calling them out for their hypocrisy. At one point, "When his family heard what was happening, they tried to take him away. 'He's out of his mind,' they said" (Mark 3:21). Mark 6:3-4 repeats the concern of his family, indicating they were offended and refused to believe in him. John 7:5 sums up James' feeling about Jesus when it says, "For even his brothers didn't believe in him."

What happened to James? How did he

become one of the leaders in the Jerusalem church? Within a few years of the Resurrection, James was "firmly embedded in the early Christian leadership in Jerusalem, as he apparently passed down the final verdict on a crucial theological discussion regarding circumcision, even though Paul, Peter, and other dignitaries were also present" (see Acts 15:13-21).[16]

Earlier, James and his mother were present in the upper room when Matthias was selected to replace Judas as an apostle (see Acts 1:14). It's believed that James was among the believers who met together at Pentecost. Something very powerful changed Jesus' brother James from being an unbelieving skeptic into one who fellowshiped with the apostles and became one of the most influential early church leaders.

POINT
TO
PONDER

Somewhere between Easter morning and the upper room, James saw the risen Jesus (as found in the creed in 1 Corinthians 15:7). James died as a martyr for his faith in the risen Lord. Other than the resurrection, what else could change James from skeptic to martyr? His transformation is Fact #5, a fifth clue in support of the Resurrection.

[16]Gary Habermas. *On the Resurrection: Evidences* (B & H Academic, 2024), page 572.

CHAPTER 12

Eventful Road Trip

Fact #6: Paul, a Jewish zealot, was radically transformed when he saw the risen Christ.

The year 1981 was wonderful for me. I enjoyed my job working as a furniture sales rep in Western Pennsylvania for Keller Manufacturing. In my spare time, I sold Shaklee Products and achieved the rank of supervisor. But the highlight of the year was the birth of our third child, Jonathan, on a sunshiny October day. As was often our practice, in December we drove to Minnesota to visit grandparents for Christmas and introduce our newest family addition to them.

A few days before Christmas, five of us loaded our luggage and Christmas presents in our 1976 Dodge Aspen station wagon. It was a great car with woodgrain siding and a hatch-back for easy access to the rear. With four-year old Joshua and three-year old Benjamin, there was still room for one of them to climb in the back behind the rear seat. For much of the drive, two-month old Jonathan was in a small bed behind the passenger seat. We started our 18-hour journey somewhere around 8 p.m., which allowed our young children to sleep most of the night. Our route took us through Ohio, Indiana, around Chicago, and then northwest on I-90. By 6:00 a.m., we had crossed into Wisconsin and were only a few hours from our final destination. And then the unexpected happened.

My wife was at the wheel. I was in the front seat peacefully holding a sleeping Jonathan in my arms. As she moved into the fast lane to pass a car, road conditions sudden-ly changed. Without warning, the roads were covered with black ice. Cars ahead of us lost control. One skidded and overturned, landing upside down on a bridge. Others slid off the road. In the midst of that chaos, we pulled over into the slow lane. The car continued sliding across the right lane, bouncing sideways down the embankment, knocking down a small road sign, and coming to a stop after bouncing off the posts of a fence that marked the edge of the highway. The car was a total loss.

Fortunately, even with the broken driver

door window and body damage, we were able to get help to push it back on the highway and drive the remaining few hours to Grandma's. Miraculously, the car hadn't overturned, as many others had, and no one was injured beside some serious bruising. And although Jonathan was in my arms when we lost control, neither one of us was injured. We were all in shock by what happened in only a few seconds. We purchased a used car to get us back home after Christmas. This was our most eventful road trip to Minnesota and one I'll never forget.

The Apostle Paul also had an eventful road trip. In my case, what happened on the way to Minnesota is something I'll never forget. In Paul's case, what happened to him on the way to Damascus was a defining moment that changed the direction of his life. Paul was a Jew and received his rabbinical education in Jerusalem. His teacher, Gamaliel, was an eminent leader in the Jewish high court and famous teacher of the Law. Paul had every reason to be proud of his heritage and accomplishments. He was a Jew by birth rather than being a converted Gentile. He was a Pharisee and upheld the strictest obedience to the Jewish law. He was zealous to honor God in everything he did, which included persecuting followers of Jesus.

Paul was present and agreed with the stoning of Stephen, the first Christian martyr, as described in Acts 7. He received permission from Jewish leaders to go to Damascus and arrest any followers and bring them back in chains to Jerusalem for punishment, imprisonment, or death. On his road trip to Damascus, Paul was blinded by a very bright light and fell to the ground. Then he heard the voice of Jesus, saying that he was the one Paul had been persecuting. A few days later, a man named Ananias came to Paul and prayed for him to regain his sight. Ananias also told Paul that God had chosen him to be his witness, telling everyone what he had seen and heard. The complete details of his conversion are described in the Acts 22.

Paul's experience on the road trip to Damascus transformed him. Prior to that trip, he was a devout Jew, intent on doing his part to eradicate the early Church. Following that trip, he became a pillar of the early Church along with Peter, Jesus' brother James, and John. His letters to churches in Ephesus, Corinth, Galatia, Rome, and others make up much of the New Testament. His faith never wavered, even though he suffered shipwreck and stoning, fled for his life at one point, and eventually died in Rome as a martyr. Paul's testimony states he met the resurrected Jesus on the road to Damascus and his life made a U-turn. How else can one explain the 180-degree change in the life of a highly-educated Pharisee and Jew? He had been intent on eliminating the church, and following his conversion, became a victim of the very persecution in which he participated.

POINT
TO
PONDER

Paul's radical transformation from a Jewish zealot to a church father and apostle sent to the Gentiles is a fact—Fact #6. When all six facts are considered together, they provide a strong argument that the Resurrection actually happened.

CHAPTER 13

Empty as
a Positive

Fact #6 + 1:
The empty tomb

When I think of the word 'empty', most of my experiences with it are negative: an empty gas tank when you have to drive somewhere; an empty stomach when there's not much food in the house; an empty checking account when there are bills to pay at the end of the month; and the feeling of emptiness after the loss of a loved one. I remember the feeling of emptiness I felt in November of 2009 when my son Joshua died.

Joshua was our first child, and his birth was viewed as an answer to prayer. He had a keen mind and a soft heart, two things that earned him both respect for his intellect and appreciation for his compassion. In November of 2000, Joshua received a diagnosis of bipolar disorder. For the next nine years, our family struggled alongside him through a frightening and uncertain journey, which ultimately caused him to lose his dream career of being a teacher. I felt grief and a huge sense of loss in seeing such a talented and God-fearing young man struggle and eventually lose his life—way, way too early. I sometimes wonder what he would have accomplished had his life not tragically ended after 32 short years.

Our family held a memorial service for him at Allegheny Center Alliance Church on Pittsburgh's Northside. There were a couple hundred people who flew in or drove hours to be there as we remembered our oldest son: his brothers and sisters, cousins, aunts and uncles, classmates, my largest furniture dealer, and my close friends Larry and Bobby. It was wonderful that so many came to express their sorrow for our loss and their appreciation for who Joshua was. But that didn't take away the emptiness I felt deep in my gut—the feeling like I'd been punched in the stomach. After a few days, I returned to work, but that emptiness lingered. It wasn't until February of the following year that I finally felt back to normal.

In contrast, there's at least one 'empty' that has a positive ring: Jesus' empty tomb. The reason Gary Habermas doesn't include it with the other six facts in support of the resurrection is because only 80% of New Testament scholars accept the empty tomb as historical fact. The other six facts are agreed upon by 96% of these scholars.[17] There is great consensus regarding the first six facts, but some question the empty tomb—thus, Habermas calls it Fact 6+1.

First, Christianity started in Jerusalem, where claims of Jesus' appearances and resurrection were first reported. It would have been impossible for the gospel to spread if his body was still in the tomb. Critics of Christianity and zealots like the pre-converted Paul would have seized the opportunity to exhume the body and prove the claims were a hoax. No one was able to produce the body. Furthermore, we have found no credible source that questions or denies the empty tomb within 100 years of the crucifixion.

Second, the action of his enemies also gives credence to an empty tomb. The empty tomb is clearly implied when the enemies of Christ claim the disciples had stolen his body. They needed to explain how it happened, so they pinned the blame on his disciples or some other followers. The body was missing.

And third, if the empty tomb was merely a concocted story and not what actually happened, it's unlikely that women would be credited as the first to discover it empty. Throughout his ministry, Jesus elevated the status of women. He spoke to the despised Samaritan woman at the well, delivered Mary Magdalene from seven demons, healed the unclean woman who touched his garment, and intervened for the woman caught in adultery. In addition to the disciples, women were among those who followed Jesus from town to town and even supported him financially (Luke 8:1-3). So it is not strange that women would be the first to find the empty tomb. But it would be strange for women to be credited with finding the empty tomb if it never happened. Women were generally considered second class citizens in the first century Roman world and in Judaism. They were held in low esteem and a woman's testimony was regarded as questionable. A man's testimony was more credible and carried more weight. For this reason, it's unlikely that the gospel accounts of women finding the empty tomb were fictional. The embarrassment factor of having women find the empty tomb is a strong indicator of its truth.

POINT
TO
PONDER

There's enough data to indicate the empty tomb
has a high probability of being true. Yet even
without this, Gary Habermas' six facts provide
strong evidence to support the conclusion that
Jesus was resurrected.

[17]Gary Habermas. *Do We Have Actual Evidence for the
Resurrection of Jesus?*, Alicia Childers Interview on YouTube,
August 12, 2022.

CHAPTER 14

Close the Sale

Decision About
the Resurrection

My paternal grandfather, Ross Ephraim Thompson, was born on January 4, 1885. He grew up on a Butler County farm, and at age 17 went to the University of Valpariso for one year of college. He returned to Butler and passed the teachers exam and began teaching school at the Ft. Sumpter school in Middlesex Township. During his first year of teaching during the 1903-04 term, Ross met Blanch Rebecca Watson. She was the new teacher at the Cunningham School, who boarded at the adjoining farm. They met, spent social time together, and were married on April 12, 1904. When that school year ended, they moved to Pittsburgh where he looked for summer employment. He found a job that paid $12 per week, going door to door collecting weekly payments from the customers of W. H. Keech Furniture Company. After a few weeks, he changed jobs and worked for the W. J. Griffith Company where he was also paid $12 per week. However, he also had the opportunity to earn a commission of 50 cents for every order that he took. He loved the idea of earning extra commissions.

Eventually he left and joined two other men who sold similar merchandise in a horse-drawn wagon in Braddock and the surrounding towns. Between 1905 and 1913, he continued to sell household goods door to door from a horse-drawn wagon. In 1918, at the age of 33, he purchased the real estate that eventually was converted into Thompson Furniture in Braddock. He improved the building in 1925, adding a fourth and fifth floor and extending it. In his memoirs, he wrote that his first experience in sales was selling a Mason jar opener door to door when he attended the University of Valpariso. He wondered if that first experience in the selling field had a major influence in his choosing a vocation where salesmanship played such an important role. Whatever started him on that career path led him to a highly successful and lucrative one.

It seems I've wanted to be in sales and marketing as long as I can remember. Maybe it's something genetic I got from my grandfather. I am drawn by the satisfaction I feel when I can use my creative juices. That inclination may explain why, as a seven-year old, I cut up a refrigerator cardboard box to create a stage for a puppet show in our living room at 1120 East End Avenue. My primary audience was my family.

My earliest recollection of being in sales was when, as a Boy Scout, Troop 23 sold Christmas trees at Koenig Field for the annual fundraiser. We sold them after Thanksgiving in the evenings and on Saturdays. Most of the actual selling was done by the adult leaders, but it required great strength and skill from the scouts to assist. Scouts would hold the tree up vertically and then spin it so interested customers could see how it looked from all sides. Once the sale was made, a scout would help carry the tree up the steps from the field and tie the tree to the car. That was my first introduction to sales and service.

In seventh grade, I ventured out on my own, selling jewelry in school. I found a hot item that appealed to a few girls in my class and some teachers: a cat's eye marble necklace. When the cat's eye marble is heated, "fried" in a skillet, and then dropped in cold water, the clear glass is crackled. The marble itself doesn't break, but the crackled glass shimmers and has astounding beauty—at least the girls and teachers thought so. It was a great seller, and I was able to sell at least ten.

We moved to 133 Gordon Street in 1960, after sixth grade. Although the street has a significant incline, our house was in a stretch that was level. Our home sat on two adjoining lots. The seven-bedroom brick house sat on one. The other lot was a level lawn. For two summers, I organized a fair in our yard with a couple other boys—Wally Futryk, Russel Malmberg, and Mark Malmberg. The fair was intended for the neighborhood kids. We sold tickets for a movie that we showed in the garage, a fishing pond, ice cones from a machine that shaved ice, popcorn with lots of butter, and several ball games with prizes. It was at the fair that I used my sizeable collection of baseball cards as prizes for the games. I wonder how much these cards from the '50s and '60s would be worth today?

By ninth grade, I moved on to a greater endeavor and was selected to participate in Junior Achievement. That in itself was an accomplishment because lots of students applied to participate. Each student, along with 15 others, was assigned to a group. Each group formed their own company, designed a product, obtained the materials needed to produce it, manufactured the product, and then sold it. Our company's creation was a beautiful wall-decor piece. The base was an 18-inch tall, diamond shaped piece of half-inch plywood, with smashed egg-shell pieces glued to it. Then a plastic stemmed rose was stapled on it. Next, it was sprayed with gold paint. Once dried, we took them home and sold them throughout the neighborhood, even to our family. What I found odd is that, in spite of its "beauty," my mother never mounted this piece of art on the living room walls—or on any other wall in the house. Somehow, it just disappeared.

While working at Thompson Furniture, I learned more about the skills needed for sales. I had worked there for a few summers as a helper when I was in high school, but moved into sales and management upon my return to Pittsburgh in 1974. As I began to work with customers, I discovered I didn't know the best way to sell our furniture. I asked my dad how to sell. His suggestion was just to give them more information. I thought there must be a better strategy to selling than that, so I contacted the NHFA furniture organization to see if there was a sales seminar I could attend.

They informed me that Charlie Gutsell, a sales trainer, was coming to Pittsburgh. I attended his seminar. He talked about effective presentations, handling objections, using trial closes, and asking for the sale. I can still hear his voice as I repeat his definition of a close: "A close is the logical conclusion to an effective sales presentation that comes naturally and simply asks for a decision without fear, fumbling, or failure."

It is my hope that I've made an effective presentation of the facts surrounding the resurrection of Jesus. Together, these facts are clues that point in one direction—that the resurrection actually happened, the deity of Jesus is clear, and Christianity is true. If these facts don't indicate the resurrection is true, then how else does one logically account for them?

For those who already trust in Jesus, my intention was to provide undeniable evidence that supports belief in the Resurrection. This knowledge may supply ammunition to fight off attacks from those who question your faith. For those who have not yet put their trust in Jesus or have walked away from the faith, my hope is that this information will encourage a re-examination of Christianity.

Sometimes hearing these facts convinces a person of the Resurrection and the truth of Christianity. Other times, people agree with the statements, but hesitate to make a decision to believe because of an emotional barrier like the hurtful actions of a significant person in our life, a painful event from the past, or even disappointment with the Church. I recognize these facts can only go so far. Ultimately, a person must trust in God and take a leap of faith.

Pastor and author Rick Warren sums it up when he says,

> While life on earth offers many choices, eternity offers only two: heaven and hell. Your relationship to God on earth will determine your relationship to him in eternity. If you learn to love and trust God's Son, Jesus,

you will be invited to spend the rest of eternity with him. On the other hand, if you reject his love, forgiveness and salvation, you will spend eternity apart from God forever . . . Just as the nine months you spent in your mother's womb were not an end in themselves but preparation for life, so this life is preparation for the next.[18]

POINT TO PONDER – ETERNITY

Is there a God? If the Resurrection occurred, then this question is answered.

If the Resurrection happened, then Christianity is true and Jesus is Lord.

If Christianity is true, then where we spend eternity hangs in the balance for each of us..

How will you respond? You can receive assurance by confessing Romans 10:9: "If you declare with your mouth that Jesus is Lord and believe in your heart that God raised him from the dead, you will be saved."

Eternity is a really long time.
A decision to follow Christ is worth it

[18]Rick Warren. *The Purpose Driven Life: What on Earth Am I Here For? (* Zondervan, 2002, 2011, 2012), pages 37, 39.

To contact Ross Thompson,
email him at the following:

rossthompson217@gmail.com